TRAVEL LIGHT
TRAVEL RIGHT

TRAVEL LIGHT
TRAVEL RIGHT

10 Tips To Make Traveling
A Better Experience

SONIKA ARRINGTON

World Traveler, Speaker, Personal Stylist
www.TravelLightTravelRightBook.com
www.Sonika360.com

WOW Book Publishing™

Dedication

I wrote this book to encourage the people who have allowed doubt, fear, time, money and other excuses to prevent them from exploring, living freely, and experiencing an incredible life.

I dedicate this book so that you will travel by every means necessary and go for your goals. You Deserve It! Live Your Life To The Fullest!! Have No Regrets and Have Fun!!! BE AMAZING...

Big Smiles,

—Sonika Arrington
World Traveler, Speaker,
Certified Personal Stylist and Author

Contents

Testimonials For

TRAVEL LIGHT
TRAVEL RIGHT

"Sonika Arrington has written a must - read and how - to guide for anyone traveling for pleasure and work . . . Read this book and learn from one of the best."

—L. Martin Pratt,
Co-founder,
Urban Literary Review & BOVTV News

"My experience traveling to Sydney, Australia with Sonika included three generations of individuals who came together to experience the history, culture and lifestyle of Australia. We ate dinner at the Sydney Tower; were mesmerized by the architect of the Sydney Opera House; sped through the city on the metro train system, toured The Blue Mountains and were enchanted with The Three Sisters. Soaked up the sun at Bondi Beach. Shopped at Patties Market and Walked thru Darling Harbor. Awesome!"

—Frances Mobley, GA

"*Sonika is an avid World traveler who knows what she is talking about. When Black Panther debuted, Sonika went to see the movie in Egypt with the locals. Who does that . . . only someone who embraces travel, the locals and adventure from a heart of love.*"

—Judith Ambrose, GA
Life Coach

"*After 9/11 I had a fear of flying, Sonika told me we were flying to St. Lucia and right away my fear & doubt kicked in. Me fly again never, but I knew she traveled a lot and knows the ins and outs on how to move around the airport and in many countries. Sonika is an A+ traveler. She made me feel comfortable, stress free, and relaxed. I am happy Sonika has introduced me to flying and traveling again. Now I travel all the time. This is a great read for everybody.*"

—Teleek Bullock, NY

"*Sonika Arrington is the absolute best people person which is an indispensable quality to have in the Travel Industry. Her customer service skills are impeccable.*"

—Taaqiy Grant,
CEO
Akhet Tours Inc.

About the Author

SONIKA IS A native New Yorker, who was born in Harlem, New York. Raised in Queensbridge Housing in Queens, New York. She is a proud mom and currently lives in Georgia, United States. She wrote this book so that you can create better travel experiences for yourself.

Sonika holds a BA in English, is a speaker, model, and certified personal stylist. Her magic power is to influence people to tune into their greatness and be true to themselves. Sonika likes to give it to you straight, keeps it real, and always has a smile. She is an advocate for the prevention and elimination of human trafficking.

Sonika travels extensively across the world and has become a connector of people, places and things that inspire greatness in all. Her adventures have led her to experience some incredible places in the world: Egypt: Cairo, Aswan, Luxor; Ghana: Accra; Nigeria: Lagos; Senegal: Dakar; South Africa: Johannesburg; Jamaica; St Lucia; British Virgin Islands: Tortola; Barbados; Canada: Niagara Falls; US: Hawaii; Thailand; Peru: Lima; Honduras: Roatan; Costa Rica; Panama; Italy: Rome, Venice; France: Paris; Netherlands:

Amsterdam; Germany: Frankfurt; Australia: Sydney; and many more magnificent places.

Sonika's motto is *"What Is For You Is For You!"*

Be authentic, inspired and know that You Are Powerful . . . Be Amazing! Learn more about Sonika at www.TravelLight TravelRightBook.com or www.Sonika360.com

Foreword

Dear Reader,

Travel Light, Travel Right is the book you need to read and learn from if you travel for pleasure or work, Sonika has a magic power to influence people and help them connect with their greatness, always with a smile.

Sonika has acquired some masterful skills and experiences by traveling extensively across the world and she will teach them to you and allow you to understand and enjoy the pleasure of traveling.

This book has the power to help you change your mind set about traveling by making it a delightful experience, it will show you how to prepare, plan and be creative. I can tell you that even being successful as I am, traveling is a big part of my life, and Sonika will teach you to enjoy it as much as I do.

Sonika has the expertise, skills, spirit and heart necessary to help you change your mind about traveling and enjoying life in the right and most powerful way.

—Vishal Morjaria
International Speaker and Award Winning Author

Acknowledgements

I GIVE THANKS AND praise to My Ancestors, My Lordship Hanuman, and My Mother Yemaya. I acknowledge the souls that are no longer with us in this physical realm Nelson Mandela, Dr Sebi, Dick Gregory, Bob Marley, Fela Kuti, Malcolm X, Garnett Silk, Frances Cress Welsing, Maya Angelou, Rosa Parks, and Harriet Tubman for having a positive impact on humanity and leading the way.

I am "GREATFUL" for the leadership of Former President Barack Obama, Oprah Winfrey, Les Brown, Queen Afua, Tony Robbins, Lauryn Hill, Sri Master Gano Grills, Etana, Ralph Smart, Kelle Edwards and many others whom I have not named but who continue to timelessly help make the world a better place for you and me.

I acknowledge some of the great business minds that I've had the pleasure of learning from and being associated with such as Bill Walsh, Kimberley S. Johnson, Vishal Morjaria, Dr. Niemah Nefertiti, L. Martin Pratt, Patricia Rogers, Adekunle Adegeye, Kenya Kicks, Coach Khayr, John Ukperegbu Kwasi Addo and Boakye Acheampong.

I acknowledge my daughter Zenobia, who is My Hope and Strength. My parents James and Deborah Arrington who are My Hero and My Rock. JahStix for keeping me standing. I acknowledge my family, friends, The JewelHunters, all my connections and relationships created throughout my travels and supporters of this book for their help in the process of writing and creating it. We Are One.

I acknowledge The Divine and My Higher Self that always assists me in my journey in life and with this book. May The Ancient Ones, The Elders, and The Ancestors continue to guide, bless, love, and protect me, my family, friends, and love ones. May we cause no harm to others and may no harm come to us. This I pray and give thanks. Finally, I acknowledge you for receiving this book and using it in the most positive way that you know. The World Is Yours To Travel!

Note to the Reader

INTRODUCTION
Travel Is An Experience

TRAVEL IS AN EXPERIENCE

Traveling—It Leaves You Speechless, Then Turns You Into A Storyteller.

—Unknown

WITH ALL THE hustle and bustle of work, children, projects, family, schedules, cleaning, school, bills, cooking, and keeping things together who has time to travel? Usually the voices in your head provide reasons why it's not possible. I mean, I want to travel one day . . . Someday I'm going to take a nice long vacation, I will travel when I retire, I can't get off from work because I don't have the time, or I have the time, but I don't have the money! He or she will not let me go or I don't have anybody to go with me. I'm just sick and tired of getting on planes and having to live out of a suitcase . . .

Any more excuses, excuses? Well, enough with the drama, worries and woeful excuses. It's time to get out, go travel, and travel better. You're not getting any younger, time waits for nobody, regardless of your income you're always going to have to pay some type of bills. I know you want something different, something new, or desire for a refresher. You have been longing for it but just haven't decided to take action.

Are you sitting at your desk in a cubicle or in the house about to cook a meal for your family? Stuck on the subway train late for work but you really don't give a damn because you don't want to be there anyway . . . Maybe you're home alone feeling sorry for yourself. I'm so tired of feeling stuck and being here. Sure, I would love to go on a girl's trip. It would be nice to take the family on a beautiful scenic road trip . . . Man, it has been a long time since I made plans to hang out with the fellas . . . I need a break from everybody and everything . . . God only knows the last time I traveled. I don't even remember the last time I traveled. I have got to plan myself some me time.

Welcome to the Land of Busyville, you stay busy doing the same thing over and over day in and day out year after year being busy, but you see there's no fun or progress living in the Land of Busyville. Tell yourself I Want More . . . go ahead say it out loud **"I WANT MORE"** I am moving out of Busyville, I am going to relax, do absolutely nothing, be still, lay on a beautiful beach, quietly listen and take in the magical sounds of the ocean as the waves caress the shore. Enjoy the moment and receive all the wonderful Vitamin D the sun has to offer. Sip a fresh coconut, so refreshing and after the flavor hits your taste buds, maybe add a little hint of rum . . . go ahead, I won't tell.

You have heard your excuses. It's either Now or Never! The Power Begins With You Right Now. Now Is The Time To Make It Happen. Make the decision. If you have decided to move forward and let go of all the excuses you have created for yourself, tell the voices in you head to *"Shut Up and Move Out Of My Way!"* I am ready to experience awesome moments greater than I can imagine. Whether you have never traveled, travel once a year for vacation or an event, or travel for a living, use these ten tips to make traveling a better experience.

Reflective Questions and Notes

What's the number one place you wish to travel to the most? Take a moment to close your eyes and think of the place you are going to travel to. Imagine being there and be specific. Write how you feel and describe all the details you want to experience.

_____

_____

_____

_____

_____

_____

_____

_____

_____

_____

_____

_____

_____

_____

_____

_____

Notes

_____

_____

_____

_____

_____

_____

_____

_____

_____

_____

_____

_____

_____

_____

_____

_____

_____

_____

Notes

_____

_____

_____

_____

_____

_____

_____

_____

_____

_____

_____

_____

_____

_____

_____

_____

_____

CHAPTER 1
Travel Light Travel Right

TIP # 1

TRAVEL LIGHT
TRAVEL RIGHT

Don't Listen To What They Say . . . Go See.

—Anonymous

TRAVEL IS AN experience which provides opportunities to learn to take in the moment. Traveling may sometimes require you to go with the flow, appreciate the big hiccups, small blessings, and allow powerful connections to appear. *Travel Light Travel Right* is the title of this book because it is a major key. Once you grasp and apply this factor, everything else will come together. When you travel light you travel right, things are in place and even if things fall apart, you are prepared to push though.

For over a decade, I have been traveling the world and have visited over forty-four countries. I have shared adventures with others, overcome lots of fears and faced many challenges. Traveling has granted me the power to build connections.

I enjoy seeing my reflection in others in return it allows you to see your reflection in me. The more I travel the more I learn to appreciate myself and my environment. In addition, to recognizing the beauty in others, there is value in having similarities and differences by culture, mannerism, beliefs, food, and beautiful places. We are all connected in some shape, form or fashion.

People are good by nature and quite interesting to watch. Get excited about traveling and the opportunities it presents for future growth and self-improvement. Focus on your behavior and not so much your appearance towards travel experience; by knowing your weakness and embracing change, you empower yourself to develop and leverage self-doubt. Improving your awareness and acting on your failures will also be a factor in building yourself.

> *You have to work just as hard to fix something as to break something.*
> *—Dustin Luther Wilkes*

My very first international travel was to Johannesburg, South Africa. I had just started working in the airline industry, invested in a passport and had seven vacation days and was about to end my shift.

Now I wasn't sure where I was going but indeed, I knew I was going somewhere. All I knew was I'm getting a stamp in my passport. I didn't have a care or worry to whom was coming with me or whom I was joining. I was just excited about going somewhere. I happened to assist and adore this wise, elder woman whom I come to call Auntie. She had a ticket problem with her flight heading to Johannesburg, South Africa. At the time, Auntie was a professor at Clarke University and we connected instantly. I asked her loads of questions about Johannesburg, the Apartheid, Mandela, the people, the food, and her home in Zimbabwe. I fell in love with the idea of going instantly. I mentioned to her, "Wow, how I would love to go!" and she replied "Come! Yes, come go with me don't worry everything would be taken care of." Now I had seven days off, but I only had two hundred and fifty dollars; yet, my heart was racing with the nervousness excitement and anticipation of wanting to go and experience it all. We exchanged information and later that night we planned out where we would stay and what we would do.

My family and friends thought I was totally crazy and suggested to make plans to travel somewhere else. I understood the worries and concerns from their reasoning why I shouldn't go by all their valid points made. They reiterated the facts that I didn't have enough money, I didn't know this woman and I've never been out of the country. Their biggest apprehension was out of all places in the world, South Africa was literally half-way around the world. The questions of what if something was to happen and how would they find me… blah, blah, blah. But all their 'ands', 'buts' and doubts went in one ear and out the other. My heart and gut feelings were in alignment to go. It felt right to me. Yes, I was nervous however this woman and I clicked. The benefit of working for the airline industry is you get to fly free. So, in my mind I was thinking "Hey this is a risk, but the risk felt right." I focused on all the good that was going to happen if I decided to go visit Africa with this African-native woman. She was willing to share and show me Africa and the opportunity was too awesome to pass up. My flight was particularly free, I had my passport ready and the time off. Who else would take me to Africa nevertheless, who else did I know that wanted to go to Africa? If something bad was going to happen then I would have to handle the situation just like if I was in the United States. So, I decided to follow through with this opportunity, let go! Let's talk about the flight- culture shock to a first-time flyer.

I was arriving late to my an eighteen-hour flight. Running to the boarding gate, I was the last passenger to board. I wasn't even sure if my tour guide was on board. Either way, I was all in and heading to The Motherland, Africa with a Business-class ticket. I thought to myself, "Well if she wasn't on board than I have a business class seat to Africa and I'm going to enjoy this trip. If all else fails, I'm going to just fly back home." Once we reached thirty-thousand feet we could walk throughout the cabin. I found her, and it was the finalization to the beginning of my adventure to Africa. The trip was truly amazing!

When I first touched down in Africa the feeling was surreal. I couldn't believe I made it. It was absolutely mind-blowing to think that little Ol' me from Queensbridge Housing Apartments in New York was in

Africa. I had her pull over to the side of the road just, so I could touch the ground and pick up some dirt. It was such an overwhelming feeling, one that I will always treasure. Everything was beautiful: the people, the place we stayed "The Afrika House" and the energy was all eye opening. The customer service was generous and outstanding. The food was simply delicious. I know I happily gained at least ten pounds because I ate everything. Auntie was the sweetest, she would not let me pay for anything, and I invested the entire two hundred and fifty dollars on gifts and souvenirs for myself, my family and friends. She showed me all of Johannesburg, we went to the Brooklyn Mall and met so many different people. It was the door-opener to my future international travels. I hold this first travel experience dear to my heart and one that I am truly Greatful to have had the pleasure to listen and follow through with my instincts. It was worth every penny and even more. I Love Africa! To see my journey through my travels, my connections with amazing people and exploring beautiful places on Earth visit www. TravelLightTravelRightBook.com or www.SONIKA360.com

Reflective Questions and Notes

Don't think about what you fear! Take control of your mind and think positive. You become what you think about. Focus on what you want. What do you want?

_____

_____

_____

_____

_____

_____

_____

_____

_____

_____

_____

_____

_____

_____

_____

_____

Notes

_____

_____

_____

_____

_____

_____

_____

_____

_____

_____

_____

_____

_____

_____

_____

_____

_____

_____

_____

_____

Reflective Questions and Notes

_____

_____

_____

_____

_____

_____

_____

_____

_____

_____

_____

_____

_____

_____

_____

_____

_____

_____

_____

_____

CHAPTER 2

Prepare And Plan

TIP # 2

PREPARE AND PLAN

If You Fail To Plan, You Are Planning To Fail.
—Benjamin Franklin

P ICK A PLACE! The world is filled with beautiful places; maybe you have a few you have always desired to explore like the pyramids in Egypt, an amazing place filled with history and adventure. Let **AKHET TOURS,** a reliable, knowledgeable, and dedicated service tour company with twenty years of experience, show you the best way to experience Egypt, contact them at www.akhettours.com. Are you brave enough to explore the exciting and cold challenge of conquering Mount Everest in Asia? Maybe you're a free spirit who loves the outdoors, longing to flow like the wind in Mount Shasta, California.

Well, get ready to spin the globe or throw your dart at the world map, it's yours for the picking. I highly recommend you get a globe and a map of the world because they are excellent resources that will improve your geography and assist your travel decisions. Hang the map in a good place for all to see and include your love ones to help choose where the next travel destination will be.

The unknown is quite interesting. Chose two different colored thumbtacks, one for the places you plan to travel and one for the places you have traveled. This is a fun way to initiate travel plans for all. Keep in mind the vision is always in where you're going.

Now that you have chosen a place and can see where it is located on the map, decide when the big date is for your travel experience. You must set your date. **Write it down . . . Write the date down . . . Write it down.** Who are you traveling with, if anybody? Are you sharing this experience with your family, friends, wife, husband, lover, coworker, a group, or even traveling by yourself? Don't worry, you are never alone, though it may feel that way . . . It's okay . . . Keep Pushing.

My mother taught me that even when you are lost, you are never alone. When you are in an unfamiliar place look for the unexpected jewels. Traveling by yourself forces you to become independent, and tune into your own powers and resources rather than those of others. It will present the opportunity for you to connect with other people that you may not normally interact with.

Make the decision become a reality with style. Are you celebrating yourself, a graduation, planning a girl's trip, renewing vows, Mardi Gras, cruise, some quiet me time, guys only, singles only, couples only, lovers weekend getaway, road trip, business trip, last minute destination, train ride, family trip, carnival in Trinidad, log cabins, trail with

Mother Nature, beach time, sailing, amusement park, sky diving, golf, camping, fishing, deep sea diving, tour guide, concert . . . Choose, Choose, Choose. Get Ready to Get Out and Do It.

Figure out how long you're staying for: a day, a weekend, a week, a month etc. Are you planning to go soon or a year from now? Are you traveling by plane, boat, train, bus, or car? Decide what is most efficient for you, how creative, and how much luxury you want to include in your travel experience. This is putting your plan into action. Part of the plan is knowing your options.

Have you ever dreamt of flying in style on a private jet? Yes, a private jet; its possible and doable check out www. netjets.com "Not only will **NetJets** change the way you fly, it will transform your sense of what's possible." Add it to your honey-do list or set of goals. Do you have a passion for the water? How about renting your own private yacht fully staffed for a day; better yet the weekend, instead of staying in a hotel, maybe book a wet, wild adventure by the sea with **REMEMBER ME NOW CHARTERS**.

Some people are not ready to commit, and some people are aching to commit. However, once you make this commitment and contract with yourself you must follow through. Come on you know you deserve it . . .

One of the most calming and refreshing places on earth to me is Maui, Hawaii. If you are given the opportunity to travel to Hawaii, go! It is a place of fresh air filled with plenty to experience: whale watching, surfing, sailing, relaxing, sunbathing. Mother nature is truly amazing when you are listening to the sounds of the ocean, absorbing the sun's rays and viewing the environment. Maui gives you the greatest feeling of peace. I made a mental contract with myself that my last breath on earth will be on Maui's beach watching the sunset. Maui is magical and quite healing. Every moment spent there is well received. Travel Light Travel Right To find out more exciting destinations to explore, visit www. TravelLightTravelRightBook.com or www.SONIKA360. com

Reflective Questions and Notes

All you need is determination and faith to accomplish any goal. People will always be skeptical but don't give up. Keep striving towards your greatness. Write down where, when, with whom, and how long your experience will be.

_____

_____

_____

_____

_____

_____

_____

_____

_____

_____

_____

_____

_____

_____

_____

_____

Notes

Notes

_____

_____

_____

_____

_____

_____

_____

_____

_____

_____

_____

_____

_____

_____

_____

_____

_____

_____

CHAPTER 3

Be Creative

TIP # 3

BE CREATIVE

You Don't Have To Be Great To Get Started But You Have To Get Started To Be Great.

—*Les Brown*

CREATE YOUR OWN pleasure! Don't be afraid to go above and beyond at treating yourself or planning to do something extra special for others. If traveling daily is part of your business living take a different route, stay at a different location, fly on another airline, rent a better car, take the ferry, take a train at least a nice one. Purchase a first-class ticket; ride in coach if you always book business class seats to rekindle the flame of appreciation and the enjoyment of success. If you currently purchase main cabin tickets, treat yourself to an upgrade and experience luxury or VIP when booking. Stay at a 5-star hotel in a suite instead of staying in a room at a 3-star hotel.

Get inspired and motivated to be surrounded by greatness and be great. If you're the boss of your company and provide the expenses for your staff's traveling, occasionally surprise them with a little extra above and beyond travel perks. Be creative make the experience better for them, book first class for the transportation and the room accommodation. My father say's *It's Nice To Be Important But It's More Important To Be Nice.*

Explore beyond your comfort zone; indulge in different kinds of food during your travel. Eat where and how the locals eat. Try fasting for a day, it helps remove waste and toxins from the body which allows you to think clearer. Do something different, be a vegan for the duration of your travels. Allow your taste buds to experience different spices and blends of food from different cultures. Maximize the taste of Mexican food, or do you just love Italian dishes? Embrace the taste of spicy Indian cuisines. Get comfortable with Soul Food or carried away with Caribbean dishes. Then savor the taste of Peruvian food or keep it authentic with Thai. If you are not innovative you are making yourself obsolete.

Shake up your scheduled travels leave on a different day or time. Experience traveling during the middle of the week, notice if there are any behavior changes. Be the first to speak. Smile, you are on candid camera and energy is contagious. Get the trip completed in three days instead of a week. You will be amazed at how much you can accomplish when pressure is applied. Face your fear and travel to the place you most want to visit, indeed there is more. Live the life you always wanted.

I celebrated a friend's 40th birthday bash in Tortola, the largest of the British Virgin Islands in the Caribbean. The celebration began with flying into St Thomas than Tortola via the ferry. I love being on the sea and look forward to every opportunity that allows me to sail. This creative adventure was enjoyed by a collective group of ten. Meeting in Tortola was a challenge because some departed on a different day and from different destinations, however, all journeys connected in Tortola where the festivals began. We drove around the island and came across Mr. Stoutt, the owner of The Stoutt Lookout. He shared some historical facts and tales of Tortola's history and its present day. He also invited us to join him for dinner where he provided all the wonderful tastes the island has to offer with all the extra trimming. The Stoutt Lookout is a happy place where everybody is considered one family and as Mr. Stoutt always shouts, "We Are One At The Lookout!"

I must mention the scenic beautiful beaches and absolute fun in the sun that surrounds the island. We took over the beach with our birthday celebration, our lively attitude, laughter, and good music. We ultimately had everyone up and dancing on their feet. Personally, the most creative experience of this celebration was the investment we shared in getting our own private yacht, 'The Friendship' then we headed to Norman Island. Our entire crew, the captain, and the staff were all black descendants and this perspective was quite interesting to me. At one point everyone went silent, you could feel the stillness that surrounded us when everyone finally took in the moment. The gentle waves, the breeze of the wind, the elements of the ocean, and the brightly sun shined upon us. It felt like time would never end. It felt like we were the celebrities featured in a music video just cruising across the water. Then I was kindly reminded of the journey my ancestors had taken before me and gave thanks to the present moment. I remember thanking them for always guiding me and being with me. It was a moment of feeling strong, humble and peaceful. As we docked into Norman Island, all eyes gazed upon us as we sailed by others.

"Watch out sheriff there was some new flavor pouring in and it was all milk chocolate"! At that moment, I felt incredibly beautiful and proud. Everybody was extremely friendly, and we stayed on the island for most of the day. Our sailing began and ended blissfully. Love and fun were expressed from the time of arrival until the final day of return. Tortola was celebrated in more ways than one. Sailing has become my new addiction. If you haven't sailed before, please give it a try; and the Carnival cruise ship doesn't apply. I suggest renting your own private yacht for a girl's trip or a day getaway with your love one. Experience something new, and share what you love to do. Make a moment for yourself, give thanks, be in love with your life and discover your creativity. To learn how to consistently make traveling creative, visit www. TravelLightTravelRightBook.com   or   www.SONIKA360. com.

Be Creative.

Reflective Questions and Notes

Let your mind begin to soar use your imagination. How can you shake things up? Do things differently? Do more than what you must do?

_____

_____

_____

_____

_____

_____

_____

_____

_____

_____

_____

_____

_____

_____

_____

Notes

_____

_____

_____

_____

_____

_____

_____

_____

_____

_____

_____

_____

_____

_____

_____

_____

_____

Notes

_____

_____

_____

_____

_____

_____

_____

_____

_____

_____

_____

_____

_____

_____

_____

_____

_____

_____

CHAPTER 4
Compare Prices

TIP # 4

COMPARE PRICES

Patience Is Bitter But It's Fruit Is Sweet.

—*Anonymous*

P RICES ARE IMPORTANT know what you want. If you haven't realized it by now, the internet is the best way to book your travel. It will provide you with anything and everything. When you're investing your hard-earned money, make sure you invest wisely. Get the most for your time and the best deals. Don't be afraid to venture and compare prices online. Online rates are generally cheaper as opposed to purchasing tickets in person or even at the last minute. Purchase your travel transportation and accommodations online.

If you're not the savvy type or just don't feel like dealing with comparing prices via the internet or in person, then invest in a good travel agent. It's important to utilize your strengths accordingly so if you must delegate . . . delegate . . . delegate. However, if you take the time to practice being patient you will discover many good deals, great discounts, special offer codes, and exclusive packages.

Airline tickets can be found greatly discounted on Mondays between the hours of midnight and 3:00am online. If you're a night owl, bored on the job from working the graveyard shift and looking for something productive to do, surf the web for low fares and great discounts. Most airline tickets purchased departing on a Wednesday rates are extremely discounted. You can find the low rates for hotel accommodations that are booked to begin during the middle of the week.

Compare the prices to flying into the same city but at a different airport. There may be more flights available. It can be cheaper, for instance to fly into Fort Lauderdale vs Miami in Florida, White Plains vs John F Kennedy or LaGuardia in New York City, Greensboro vs Raleigh in North Carolina, Midway vs O'Hare in Chicago, Orange County vs Los Angeles in California and many others. Compare taking the train on Amtrak versus taking the bus on Greyhound. Compare competitors like Mega Bus or the China Bus, if you don't want to fly. Look at the prices and remember to look for and use offer codes for renting cars through car rental agencies like Hertz, Enterprise, Budget or National. The prices may be even lower when you book through third party affiliations like Hotwire, Booking Buddy, Expedia, or Orbitz but be mindful and watch out for the fine print when it comes to making changes.

For comparing hotel and room accommodations checkout Air BNB, they have great prices and lodging worldwide. Give hostels a whirl. Read the reviews and share your review after your experience with your transportation, lodging, and restaurant. Sharing is caring. This keeps others informed and helps spread the knowledge and experience of travels whether it was a pleasurable delight or a total discomfort.

Be aware of rates around holidays, spring break, and the summertime. Prices are increased during peak seasons, so check your calendar dates and evaluate if you want to travel in the high peak season or during the off-peak season. The summertime and spring break are considered high peak travel season so be patient and give yourself extra time. You will encounter plenty of unaccompanied minors and young adult spring break travelers creating heavy traffic during this time of travel, so prepare accordingly. In the summertime, there are more delays due to weather like thunderstorms, lightning and remember the airlines are not responsible for Mother Nature. You go on vacation to refresh, so practice being patience.

Through the mist of preparing, it's important to know what you want to discover. To get three generations: grandmother, mother and daughter to travel to Sydney, Australia was a little tricky for me because my mother has been battling issues with her leg. We worried about her comfortability and endurance during the nineteen-hour duration of the flight. The initial itinerary my friend created for the trip would be quite challenging for my mom because it was too much traveling at once. So, I compared prices for hotels and flights and was successful in creating an additional plan to get her to Sydney, Australia. I added extra days to our itinerary, so the total duration was spilt up. The first day I flew my mother from North Carolina to Atlanta, Georgia. The next day we all flew to our connecting location of Los Angeles, California and stayed a day there. My mom was well rested for her first journey of a fourteen-hour flight. I was very proud of her because she pushed through and successfully made it to and from Sydney without any problems. One tip for long distance traveling is to use compression socks because it can reduce swelling, it's always a great tool to have.

Once we arrived in Sydney, we met up with the remaining grandmothers, mothers and daughters of our group. We explored Sydney through shopping at Patties Market Place, dinner at Sydney Tower Eye. It has a phenomenal skyline view of Sydney unfortunately the food was displeasing. But I will mention that the manager went above and beyond to make things right for us by offering an additional complimentary dinner for the next day, however we declined because our itinerary was full. We explored Sydney through a hop-on-hop-off pass, which gave us entry to the Opera House, Taronga Zoo, Sea Life Aquarium. We did get to experience being on the water with a cruise liner that took us under Sydney Harbour Bridge which was built into our package. We toured Blue Mountains National Park where we learned about the legend of The Three Sisters. Australia was awesome, and well worth the wait for practicing patience on a long flight. Discover traveling through varies pricing packages, visit www.TravelLightTravelRightBook.com or www.SONIKA360.com.

Reflective Questions and Notes

How will you to get to your destination? What fears do you have about reaching your destination? List how and why you must face your fears and push through.

_____

_____

_____

_____

_____

_____

_____

_____

_____

_____

_____

_____

_____

_____

_____

_____

Notes

_____

_____

_____

_____

_____

_____

_____

_____

_____

_____

_____

_____

_____

_____

_____

_____

_____

_____

_____

Notes

_____

_____

_____

_____

_____

_____

_____

_____

_____

_____

_____

_____

_____

_____

_____

_____

_____

_____

_____

CHAPTER 5

Stay Ready And Research

TIP # 5

STAY READY AND RESEARCH

If You Stay Ready You Don't Ever Have To Get Ready.
—Will Smith

HERE'S HOW TO beat the bumper to bumper traffic and never-ending lines. In most big city airports, the busiest days to fly are usually Mondays and Tuesdays due to all the business travelers. To avoid the lines at the airport, research TSA Pre Check, CLEAR, and Global Entry. All three programs will allow you to move either through airport security lines faster, prevent you from repacking your bag, reduce the strip and search procedure or allow you to reenter the country when traveling internationally instead of coming through long lines at customs and immigration. All are absolute time savers.

TSA Pre-Check allows for expedited screening at participating airports. In addition, passengers twelve and younger are allowed through TSA Pre-Check lanes with eligible passengers. Others traveling, family members thirteen and older, must go through the standard security lanes. This policy only applies to TSA Pre-Check program.

Take Uber or Lyft to the airport to avoid high paying parking fees or take public transportation. Always arrive at least two hours before your flight if you are going to be flying international and at least one hour before your flight if flying domestic and checking bags. Most airlines offer discounts or free baggage for obtaining their credit cards or joining their miles program.

Check in for your flight on your cell phone using the mobile app or have your boarding pass printed at home or from the hotel to avoid standing in lines. Bring an extra pair of socks if you're wearing sandals, open shoes, or no socks to prevent from having to walk on the floors barefoot when going through the metal detectors at the airport security screening.

Research where you plan to visit and set up great activities to do while you are there. State your requests in your reservation or travel package, for example, a vegetarian meal, the use of a wheelchair, medical device, portable oxygen concentrator, respirators, nebulizers, CPAP, have a lap child, an unaccompanied minor, a service animal, or an emotional support animal.

If you choose to use the Unaccompanied Minor program, where underage children get to experience traveling without you, but are escorted and monitored by staff for a fee, research the company's policy. This program usually provides a service for minors to safely travel to and from their destination if you are not able to travel with them. If you want to send your child or children across the country or down south to visit the grandparents while you get to enjoy a private vacation this is worth the investment to gain some me time. The fees and ages of the child or children vary between companies so do your homework.

If you have a pet, it may be allowed to travel with you as well. Airlines have fees to allow your pet to fly in the cabin with you in the animal's kennel depending of the size of the animal or may be allowed to fly in the cargo section. Research the policy and requirements for pet travel. Check for embargos when animals are not allowed to fly due to extreme weather conditions. Research airlines' rules and regulations, especially if you are bringing your pets to travel internationally, they may need vaccinations and quarantines. If you are traveling active duty on orders in the military and bringing your pet, make sure to have the correct documentation. It's better to be prepared, and safe during your travels. Some airlines also provide active duty military free bags at check-in so ask questions.

Get A PASSPORT Now! I repeat if you do not have a passport get one as soon as possible, even if your international plans are not soon. It's better to have one and not need it rather than to need it but not have one. It will cost you extra money to have it expedited. If you currently have a **passport,** make sure it is **not** going to **expire** within the next **six months** of your travel; many places will not accept a passport as a valid form of documentation if its going to expire within six months. Make copies of your passport and keep them in a safe place or with someone you trust who is reliable and make sure you have memorized their telephone number, especially when traveling abroad.

Double-check and verify you have the appropriate visas, and other paperwork necessary for travel, such as your marriage license or divorce papers if your name has changed. Lastly, always verify that the name on the reservation matches the same name on your valid identification.

Long before I realized, my ancestors were leading the way for me to travel back to the Middle Passage. I have traveled to many parts of Africa but going to Ghana was special. Throughout the process of retracing my roots, I always thought it was going to be traced back to Nigeria or Ghana. African Ancestry administered my matriclan analysis and the results were the Yoruba and Fulani people living in

Nigeria. The results helped explain my initial personal connection to the Yoruba culture. I've always been joked from my African friends that "You're more African than me." I was set to go to explore Ghana with a good friend whom had already visited several times. However, on the day of the trip she didn't realize her visa to Ghana had expired and she was not permitted to board the flight. She had to delay her travels until her documentation was updated. So, I proceeded off to Ghana by myself even though I am never alone.

When I arrived, I had another friend who lived there pick me up and showed me around. I met with a seventy-two-year-old herbalist, yet he could pass for a fifty-two-year-old. He shared so much information about the body's health:

digestion, circulation and the power of herbs and plants: moringa, the bitter leaf, and almond trees. I got to help prepare the food that evening and felt right at home. Once my friend arrived, we headed to Cape Coast Castles. Upon entering the castle, I met some enchanting little boys who had me laughing and teaching me the latest dances; they were so humble and inspiring. Once inside Cape Coast Castles, I explored the male slave dungeons, the female slave dungeons, the master's quarter and the Door of No Return. I would love to share my thoughts in detail except I will leave you with an inspiring caption from a plaque on the wall of Cape Coast Castle.

In Everlasting Memory of the Anguish of Our Ancestors.

May Those Who Died Rest In Peace.

May Those Who Return Find Their Roots.

May Humanity Never Again Perpetrate Such Injustice Against Humanity.

We, The Living, Vow To Uphold This.

I highly and strongly encourage YOU to go, explore, experience, and feel for yourself. It is a

MUST on my list. However, if you can't get there, check out the movie "Sankofa" from 1993. If you are looking for a place to lodge once at Cape Coast stay at the lovely place, One Africa Health Resort. It's right on the Atlantic Ocean with gorgeous cultural chalets, friendly staff and has a timeless museum. The vegetarian food and fish cuisines were delicious. You are sure to feel the love. Squeeze in some time to visit Kakum National Park while in Cape Coast. I faced my fear of walking the rope canopy walkway.

Ghana is one of my favorite places to visit in Africa. I'm always ready to go to Ghana. Once you do your research you will too.

Stay Ready And Research.

Visit my websites www.TravelLightTravelRightBook.com or www.SONIKA360.com to learn about upcoming travel tours and events.

> *If people like you, they'll listen to you, but if they trust you, they'll do business with you.*
> —*Zig Ziglar*

Reflective Questions and Notes

Be mindful of your words. Do you hold yourself accountable for your thoughts and actions? How do you stay ready and prepared? Through research you can prepare and improve. Begin your journey now.

_____

_____

_____

_____

_____

_____

_____

_____

_____

_____

_____

_____

_____

_____

Notes

_____

_____

_____

_____

_____

_____

_____

_____

_____

_____

_____

_____

_____

_____

_____

_____

_____

_____

_____

_____

_____

Notes

_____

_____

_____

_____

_____

_____

_____

_____

_____

_____

_____

_____

_____

_____

_____

_____

_____

CHAPTER 6
Do Your Budget

TIP # 6

DO YOUR BUDGET

What Is For You Is For You.

—*Sonika Arrington*

D ECIDE WHAT YOU can afford for your travel and aim to stick to your budget. Calculate your prices and round up. When you round up the price you stay within your budget and remain on the safe side. For example, if that personal spa costs $117.00 dollars round it up as $120.00 dollars and by doing so it will give you some extra leverage for any big hiccups that may occur.

Set a goal to spend during your travels and decide the amount each family member will be given. Give your child an allowance to spend during the trip for him or her to purchase any cool item or gift that their little heart desires throughout the trip. Let them know once the amount is spent, they will not be given any more money. This will keep them accountable for their spending and make them responsible for their decisions and actions. This instils the ability to master their managing skills as well as respect the value of a dollar or monetary transactions. This process keeps things within expectations. You must follow through and stick to your decisions and by doing so your values and actions will line up.

Bill Walsh, CEO of **Powerteam International** always says *"Go VIP Or Go Home"* and indeed I have learned how true this is in more ways than one. I would add when going VIP, go all the way. It's different at the top because it feels better and there's more room. However, if your financial plan isn't at VIP status then stick to coach or main cabin. Kudos to you, on understanding your pockets. Keep pushing yourself to VIP status. Stay True to Yourself!

If you can afford and want to invest into the luxury of VIP . . . enjoy! You absolutely deserve it! Make sure you ask for all the details involved with the perks. For example, business class, first class cabin, 5-star suites, yachts, exclusive packages, bonuses and other excellent offers available. Remember, don't count the moments make the moments count.

When doing your budget always remember to inquire about military rate, AARP discounts, interline prices, early-bird specials, or last-minute deals. If you decide to take a cruise at the last minute, often cruise lines will give incredible discounts and deals to fill the ship. This option for planning to purchase last-minute cabins can work in your favor. Look for interesting middle of the week sails during off peak season for quick cruises and last-minute getaways. You are sure to grab great deals.

If traveling with a group, check for group rates as well as discuss dining tips, room occupancy accommodations and arrangements before traveling to prevent having any unexpected add-ons to your bill and budget.

I was fortunate to have been invited to stay at my friend's home in Dakar, Senegal. From the moment, I landed in Dakar I was smitten by the huge beautiful bronze statue of a family called "The

African Renaissance Monument". As we drove through the city, I can remember thinking my roots are not from here because everybody was so tall. I recall having to look up to people that I got to connect with. I purchased tons of beautiful fabric, artifacts, jewelry, and fell in love with the Yassa Chicken. I was surprised how the music was infused with Afro-Cuban sounds. I was awed how couples were doing tango-like dances and were in love with each other and dancing. I enjoyed the live band and we had the time of our life. Music brings people together. At Lac Rose, I scooped up pink water to bring back home, I referred to it as the Pink Lake. To Goree Island we had to take a ferry over, where the Atlantic slave trade took place. There I toured the House of Slaves and passed through the Door of No Return. Dakar, Senegal was outstanding, and I enjoyed feeling like royalty.

Join me on my website: www.TravelLightTravelRightBook. com or www.SONIKA360.com to share more about this chapter, my book, and other additional material to improve your budget for traveling.

Reflective Questions and Notes

How much do you want to invest on your travel? Do what you can afford and don't worry about others. Invest in yourself and bring value to others.

Notes

_____

_____

_____

_____

_____

_____

_____

_____

_____

_____

_____

_____

_____

_____

_____

_____

_____

Notes

_____

_____

_____

_____

_____

_____

_____

_____

_____

_____

_____

_____

_____

_____

_____

_____

_____

CHAPTER 7

How To Deal With Unexpected Problems In Travel

TIP # 7

HOW TO DEAL WITH THE UNEXPECTED PROBLEMS IN TRAVEL

I Love Places That Make You Realize How Tiny You And Your Problems Are.

—*Anonymous*

THINGS WILL NOT always go as perfectly planned and your behavior never lies. You will discover more about yourself in times of crisis. Focus on the positive side and move forward. Whether you are traveling by plane, train, boat, bus, or car errors and unexpected problems may happen. How to handle things when they fall apart and out of place. Take a deep breath, maybe a couple, depending on the situation. Breathing is essential and allows you to think better during a time of crisis. Keep calm, cool and listen instead of just reacting. You will be able to receive a better and brighter solution to the problem when you focus on finding a solution rather than wasting your time and energy in complaining about the problem.

You will get things resolved quickly when you are in control of your actions and mannerisms because yelling at someone who can potentially help you will only delay your process and will not work in your favor. The energy you put out the more you get back. Your communication skills are crucial. Avoid being rude and disrespectful to others. Pay attention to your surroundings. **Read . . . Read . . . Read**! Reading is fundamental.

You missed your flight! The plane is right there! The agent will not open the door for you to board! Guess what the positive side is, you're now early for the next flight. Yes, the agent closed the door right in your face. It is part of the FAA's policy and they cannot and will not hold the flight unless they are instructed to do so. They are not allowed to hold flights even if they know your arrival plane is the reason for your delay. Don't be rude to the agent, instead proceed quickly to find a better way to get rebooked or rerouted to your destination.

You are speeding down the road and caught a flat tire. It's okay, you have AAA, so your tire will get fixed. You're safe and still alive. The flat tire protected you from getting into a major car accident. Also, the flat tire may have slowed you down and prevented you from getting a speeding violation and points against your driver's record.

You missed your cruise ship. I bet you will never do that again; lesson learned. Leave a day early before your scheduled ship departs if you have more days to play with. You booked the wrong train ticket enjoy the new scenic ride, maybe your services are needed along this new train ride instead. You couldn't board the bus you purchased your ticket for because there weren't enough seats. Be early next time. You are destined to meet, connect or help someone along the new route.

Someone is sitting in your seat; take action, be polite and mind your manners. We have all made mistakes, be kind and thoughtful. You are a very large person and you know you will take up two seats please purchase two tickets it will avoid the stress on you as well as the person having to adjust next to you.

Be responsible for your actions and keep the company accountable for their failures. Use the power of the pen to send thankful letters regarding all the positive and great customer service you received during your travels. Always follow up with a letter mailed, faxed, email, or telephone call about your situation regarding any inconveniences and state what it is you're requesting as compensation. The power of the pen is priceless. It's not the end of the world, though it may feel that way. Remember to breathe, look for the positive side of things, learn the lesson, be polite and think of the next safest, quickest and most affordable way to reroute you to your destination.

Focus on creating a solution; the more you waste your energy on the problem the longer you're stuck in a state of mind where you're feeling angry, horrible, and depressed. Everything has its place in time. You create your future by how you respond to your present.

My daughter's first international request was Paris, France. I gladly invested in giving her the birthday gift of visiting Paris, as I also love to shop. My friend and her daughter also joined us. I would recommend that you invest in Rosetta Stone French lessons, travel with a French-speaking person or download the translator app on your phone. French is the dominant language. On more than one occasion we were encouraged to speak French. Once we landed, we asked the information clerk for directions to our hotel, The Holiday Inn. She kindly responded, "French, Mademoiselle, French!" and I laughed it off and said to my daughter, "Dorothy, we aren't in Kansas anymore". Even with our French-speaking inabilities, we made it safely to the hotel and were bold enough to take the Paris Metro System to explore the city of Paris.

We went to the Eiffel Tower and my daughter challenged me to walk to the top with her. When I looked down, I was so scared, yet I had no other choice but to keep pushing to the top and was elated when we made it. At the top the view was spectacular, and the entire city looked beautiful lit up. I got to shop at the Chatelet Mall. Did lots of touring and site seeing. The unexpected problem arose when we were returning to the States. The flight was full, everybody was assigned a seat except for me and from the looks of things I was going to be left in Paris. I would have to separate from my daughter and wait another day to return to the United States. I didn't panic or get upset but I did take a lot of deep breaths. I was about to give up and make other arrangements for my daughter to travel with my friend but as I always say I'm never alone. I focused on making the flight back home and within twenty minutes of the flight there were ten people missing from a connecting flight which allowed me to board. I quickly hopped on the bus from the gate and was escorted to the plane. We were all greatful for that moment. I am always giving thanks because things continue to work in my favor whenever I travel. How To Deal With Unexpected Problems In Travel Discover how to connect with people, places, and things. Visit www.TravelLightTravelRightBook.com and www.SONIKA360.com.

Reflective Questions and Notes

Remember to Breathe. How do you handle unexpected problems? What can you do to find better solutions to your problems?

_____

_____

_____

_____

_____

_____

_____

_____

_____

_____

_____

_____

_____

_____

_____

Notes

_____

_____

_____

_____

_____

_____

_____

_____

_____

_____

_____

_____

_____

_____

_____

_____

_____

_____

Notes

CHAPTER 8
Priceless Packing

TIP # 8

PRICELESS PACKING

If You Wish To Travel Far and Fast, Travel Light.
—*Cesare Pavese*

WHAT TO PACK? You're overwhelmed with getting ready for the big trip. Things are finally lining up and the big day is approaching. You get so excited that you lose your sense of reasoning and end up over packing. Now your bags are filled and overflowing with unnecessary things. Well, here are some tips to make your packing easy.

Pack similar, color-coordinated outfits to match each other to prevent the need of having to bring so many different color shoes. Bring a comfortable pair of shoes and a pair of flip flops. Include a light-weight jacket or a shawl, lightweight jeans or pants, a light towel, and sometimes your favorite blanket, basic first aid kit, and a book that you have been planning to read. Remember to pack your charger and if traveling international bring a portable convertor outlet.

When packing, roll your clothes instead of folding them. Purchase 3.4 oz travel size toiletries which are the recommended travel size amount for liquids. If you are traveling with more than one person, designate one suitcase to store all the oversized liquid items. For example, large mouthwash, toothpaste, hair gel, shampoo, conditioner, shaving cream, sunscreen, perfume, lotion, baby oil, or that bottle of rum, etc.

I prefer **not** to check any bags especially if you're traveling for a week or less. Bring carry-on instead and save your money from the baggage fees to spend on something else. Make sure your checked bag does not weigh more than 50 pounds; otherwise, you will be subject to paying additional over-weight baggage fees. Make sure your luggage is not oversized because airlines will charge additional fees. Check the baggage allowance for bags, especially when traveling international.

You may also wait to purchase your toiletries at your destination and give them to the residents when you are returning. Leave room for shopping, you can purchase new items from abroad and use them as souvenirs and keepsakes. Research their fashion trends and purchase some needed items there. You may be able to do some haggling and exchange your old clothes for their new items. You may be able to give the things you don't need away to the locals and have more space for cool new things from your travels. Donate your clothes or unwanted items to the locals. It's a great deed, and you're helping somebody that may be less fortunate.

Haggling can be fun and is a way to develop relationships. Stand your ground and ask for what you want. Learn basic words and phrases in the native language of the country or area you are traveling to. When locals notice you have attempted to learn the language it is very appreciated. Rosetta Stone works. Make friends with the residents, they are more than willing to share the pros and cons of places to visit and what to avoid. Ask more than one person. Always pay attention and listen to your inner voice.

Don't get caught up with buying souvenirs for everybody. Keep it simple, light and reasonable. Purchase a bunch of different key chains or magnets because t-shirts and mugs for everybody can become expensive and add to baggage weight. They should have been there to experience it for themselves. Lastly, make sure to use bank cards with no international fees when making charges aboard.

'Jamaica, Land We Love!' Wow, I've lost track of the amount of times I've explore this adorable island country! The very first time flying into Jamaica was a surreal moment. Upon landing, the clouds split like your entering the Gates of Heaven over the mountain tops. Looking for Heaven on Earth, well look no farther, it's in Jamaica. Jamaica is infused with respect, love, and good moments spent here with the native people, family, friends, loved ones, and business partners. You can expect to hear the best reggae music; my favorite female reggae artist Etana, Beloved Garnett Silk, and Legendary Bob Marley.

To complete all its' giving, Jamaica has ackee with salt fish, jerk chicken, red snapper, Appleton Rum, and herbs. You leave feeling 'Alright'! You are ready to travel better! Go to my website now: www.TravelLightTravelRightBook.com and www.SONIKA360. com

Reflective Questions and Notes

Travel light and travel right. Do you know how and what to pack? Do not over pack and bring comfortable footwear. Remember to bring a book because reading is fundamental.

_____

_____

_____

_____

_____

_____

_____

_____

_____

_____

_____

_____

_____

_____

_____

_____

Notes

_____

_____

_____

_____

_____

_____

_____

_____

_____

_____

_____

_____

_____

_____

_____

_____

_____

_____

Notes

_____

_____

_____

_____

_____

_____

_____

_____

_____

_____

_____

_____

_____

_____

_____

_____

_____

_____

CHAPTER 9

Ask Questions &
Add Tips And Treats

TIP # 9

ASK QUESTIONS &
ADD TIPS AND TREATS

The More That You Read, The More Things You Will Know. The More That You Learn, The More Places You'll Go.

—Dr. Seuss

N O QUESTION IS a dumb question. If you are unsure or don't understand something, always ask! It can help save time. If you don't ask, you will never know. Speak even if your voice shakes. If at anytime throughout your travel experience you see something that appears to be off or triggers your senses that something is wrong or doesn't feel right, trust your instincts because 9 out of 10 times your senses don't lie.

I am passionate about the prevention of human trafficking. "*Human Trafficking is the recruitment, transportation, transfer, harboring or receipt of persons: by the threat or use of kidnapping, force, fraud, deception or coercion, or by the giving or receiving of unlawful payments or benefits to achieve the consent of a person having control over another person, and for the purpose of sexual exploitation or forced labor."* I challenge you to ask questions and pay attention to your surroundings when traveling. Follow through in trusting your instincts and together, if you see something say something; you can help stop and prevent sex trafficking.

Children all over the world are being targeted at an alarming rate by people pimping them out and getting them hooked on drugs, or in some cases made to live as slaves with false hopes or becoming citizens. If it does not look right, or feel right, it just might not be right. For more information check out www.humantrafficking.org. If you or someone you know is a victim of human trafficking call 1-888-373-7888 or text 233733. Raise Your Awareness!

Question it! It's better to save a life and prevent an act of harm from being committed on someone. It's a wonderful feeling to know that just because you took the time to ask a question you may have prevented a horrible situation from taking place. Let's read, pay attention, listen, watch and speak up for yourself and for others when traveling.

"Closed mouths don't get fed." If there is anything you want to happen during your experience let it be known. Always ask for an upgrade. You want an early check in or late check out . . . ask for it! You want to move your seat . . . ask for it! You want to take an early or later flight . . . ask for it! You are not satisfied with your cabin accommodations or the service was horrible . . . speak up! You're standing in a very long line, need to get through airport security fast, ask everyone if

you may kindly skip the line because you need to catch your departing flight. You will be surprised that there are plenty of nice and thoughtful people in the world.

You will notice eight out of ten times, when you ask for what you want you will receive it. It's not so much what you do, but rather how you do things. Give and share specific details in regarding everything you want or need. Please use your manners. **"Please and Thank You"** are Powerful Words, use them often. Smiles and niceness are keys that go along way; practice makes perfection.

Remember to be thoughtful of others, give tips and treats. Carry a snack for yourself and an extra snack for someone special you encounter during your journey as a little gift. Appreciate the small blessings and sweet little gestures as well as the big ones. Give honest compliments to both men and women. Spread love and positivity. It comes back to you ten-fold.

Pay it forward. Travel with five dollars gift cards to express your gratitude when someone does something nice for you or has gone above and beyond to make your travel experience better. Get a prepaid gift card for coffee, a meal, or a shopping store. Everyone loves sweet surprises. Carry some chocolate; it's a great way to spread the love and the thanks.

Be an ordinary person who does extraordinary things and observe how your travels become enriched with enjoyment as you enrich the lives of others. You experienced outstanding service, leave a monetary tip even if they aren't allowed to take it. Leave it on the counter or in a discreet place. Tip those that get forgotten or least don't expect to get a tip, such as custodial employees and housekeeping employees. Please remember to tip your wheelchair pusher.

Offer to purchase a drink for the person sitting next to you. Have your personal prepaid gift card with your business logo attached on it and loaded with twenty dollars. This will create a moment in someone's memory that will last a long time and the feeling you share is priceless. The additional bonus is you're building your business and promoting self-advertisement while traveling. This person is going to share and tell everybody about your act of kindness. Little surprises go a long way.

If you love going to the spa, well one of the best places on earth that specialize in giving body massages is Thailand. At a fraction of the cost, I experienced the best spa body treatment in my life. The spa service wins hands down in Thailand. I loved going to the spa, it became a new addiction! Make sure while you're there, indulge in a massage and body treatment daily at the low rate of roughly twenty-five dollars. Our visit to Thailand included a group of twelve woman. We were constantly asked to take pictures with the natives as they were so engrossed with our Beauty. We went extreme-shopping; bring an empty suitcase because mostly everything is inexpensive. You will quickly fill your suitcase with jewelry, bags, clothes, electronics, etc. At very low prices, skies the limit of what you can purchase. Enjoy the sites, everything is amazing! You well be surrounded by the presence of the Great Buddha and all the marvelous temples. The locals are exceptionally friendly and helpful. The lengthy journey from the states is well worth the experience in Thailand. Have fun! If you forget to bring your camera, don't worry you can by the same one there for half the price. Go VIP all the way and gladly tip big. Fill your journey with moments that last a lifetime-visit www.TravelLightTravelRightBook.com and www.SONIKA360. com.

Reflective Questions and Notes

People will always remember how you made them feel. Go out of your way to please or surprise someone. What are ways you are going to make others feel good?

_____

_____

_____

_____

_____

_____

_____

_____

_____

_____

_____

_____

_____

_____

_____

_____

Notes

_____

_____

_____

_____

_____

_____

_____

_____

_____

_____

_____

_____

_____

_____

_____

_____

_____

_____

Notes

_____

_____

_____

_____

_____

_____

_____

_____

_____

_____

_____

_____

_____

_____

_____

_____

_____

_____

CHAPTER 10

Have Fun,
You Deserve It

TIP # 10

HAVE FUN, YOU DESERVE IT

May I See Beautiful Things And May Only Beautiful Things See Me.

—*Sonika Arrington*

HAPPINESS IS ENJOYING the joy of living, loving and being loved. Prosperity is having success and the abundance of wants and needs. Treat yourself. You are entitled to the blessings that you desire! Know that you deserve it. Create the funding for your vacations by circulating and investing your money. Have Fun!

Time to travel, you are great, powerful and divine. Making traveling a better experience by planes, trains, boats, buses, cars and even your feet you are sure to go far. Enjoy each minute and every moment. Life is what you make it. Make the moments count because it does not last. Experience new things and connect with different people. Go where you dare to travel. Share the fun with your loved ones and encourage others to travel. Have no regrets and learn to appreciate the lessons quickly, safely and more importantly, respectfully.

Go for the gold, do it big and go all the way. Know that you deserve only the best and do it your way. It is true that little surprises go along way. Never settle and live your life to the fullest. Seek for the positivity, if a mistake is made, it's okay. Be kind to others, be polite to others, and be mindful of the power of your words and actions. Recognize there is a time to work and there is a time to play.

Growth is the purpose, everything else is the result.
                                                    —Coach Khayr.

The most important investment is yourself . . . You deserve to explore Egypt. Egypt is not a trip, it is an experience. You are never too old to learn and you are never too young to teach. Grab your passport and grab a friend. Experience the Nile River, The Pyramids of Giza, and the Sphinx. Go visit the Step Pyramid of the Pharaoh Zoser and the Cairo Museum. Continue your journey to Abu Simbel and visit the fabulous mortuary Temples of Ramses II and Nefertari. Journey to the West Bank and visit the mortuary Temples of Hatsheput and the Valley of The Kings.

Why wait any longer explore and experience the powers of Egypt. I followed my passion for travel and it led me to Egypt. You can as well, check out www.akhettours.com This tour company will make your experience to Egypt the best it can be. This world is filled with incredible people, get to know each other. Stay true to yourself and listen to your inner voice. Give thanks for the beautiful places you travel to. Things are meant to be explored.

Whether you do it once or twice, or, as often as you like go see plenty sites. Enjoy your travels and connect with people, places and things. Make away even if there appears to be no way. You are more powerful that you think. Some may try to stop you but stand on your own two feet. What Is For You Is for You. Travel Light Travel Right Life is amazing. Blowing you all big smiles. Love to travel is what you do now.

Have Fun, You Deserve It

See you in the skies or a foreign place but until then, be safe . . .

Now go to my website, yes, the travel place.

www.TravelLightTravelRightBook.com or
www.SONIKA360.com

Reflective Questions and Notes

I know you want a stamp in your passport. List all the places you are going to visit. What do you deserve? Winners never quit.

_____

_____

_____

_____

_____

_____

_____

_____

_____

_____

_____

_____

_____

_____

_____

_____

_____

_____

Notes

_____

_____

_____

_____

_____

_____

_____

_____

_____

_____

_____

_____

_____

_____

_____

_____

_____

_____

Notes

_____

_____

_____

_____

_____

_____

_____

_____

_____

_____

_____

_____

_____

_____

_____

_____

_____

_____

Purchase your 2019 Calendars NOW!

EXPLORE

Sonika Arrington
The Positivty Queen

For more than a decade, Sonika Arrington has been a World-Traveler and connector of people, places, and things. She has traveled to over forty-four countries and still loves to travel. She is an author, speaker on positive thinking, model, and a certified personal stylist. With a BA in English, she is a proud mom and an advocate for the prevention of human trafficking. Her magic power is to influence people to tune in to their greatness and be true to themselves. As a result, you feel authentic and strong. Sonika likes to keep it real, give it to you straight, and always with a smile.

EXPLODE

51547893R00076

Made in the USA
Columbia, SC
22 February 2019